The Fertile Land

The Fertile Land

a symphony in six parts for soloist and orchestra

DATO MAGRADZE

THIS IS A GENUINE RB EDITIONS BOOK

Rare Bird Books
453 South Spring Street, Suite 302
Los Angeles, CA 90013
rarebirdlit.com

Copyright © 2021 by Dato Magradze

Translated from the Italian by Gabriel Griffin

FIRST NORTH AMERICAN TRADE PAPERBACK ORIGINAL EDITION

All rights reserved, including the right to reproduce this book or portions thereof in any form whatsoever, including but not limited to print, audio, and electronic. For more information, address:

Rare Bird Books Subsidiary Rights Department
453 South Spring Street, Suite 302
Los Angeles, CA 90013

Set in Dante
Printed in the United States

10 9 8 7 6 5 4 3 2 1

Publisher's Cataloging-in-Publication Data available upon request.

To the luminous memory of Georgia's great writer
Otar Chkheidze, who gave us, along with other masterpieces,
the translation of *The Waste Land* by T. S.Eliot.

1. *The Needle's Eye Triumphant Arc (A# minor)*

Give me a moment
to lose myself far away,
so I may delight in life and love
and return, like Ulysses, to you.

I would buy the world for a penny,
trace a blank sheet with a pen,
and with deference, be present
at the burial of the moment in time.

I have no intention of weeping,
nor do I see my neighbour's corpse before me,
but simply recognise the scene
of the burial of the Count of Orgaz.

Rather than chanting farewell verses
I've preferred gay refrains,
and I'd give my life to save you,
though I should be rattling my bones.

When verses are self-sufficient
and fly the flag of poetry,
a stanza budding from a corpse
summons may-bells from fossil wood.

I found the words I wished to say
though the garden of Gethsemane trembled;
while the poet strives, there opens before him
the needle eye's Triumphal Arc.

I ask you please to note
that the Georgian police eavesdrop on me
because I will not be silent, and
as for the Security guards,
I get them to read my poems.
They intercept my phone calls,
investigating whoever stands by me.
Ever since I became aware
of the needle eye's Triumphal Arc

I became the focus of their interest
and they continually worry
over who stands behind me.

I tell them: the one you're searching for
you'll see only if you have faith.
-if I don't believe, I won't see him
-if you don't see, you won't believe him.
The reason of this difference
is what the eavesdropping SSS is investigating,
but nothing will make me be silent.

I did not keep quiet when the sailors
mocked the albatross—the king of the skie—
when clumsily lurching over the deck
they placed a pipe in its beak.

I was not silent when the customs officers
impounded the poet's "Drunken Boat."
Refusing such a cargo,
he renounced this waste land
and roamed the high seas.

Nor did I keep silent when
my country plunged into misfortune
and public officials in the forest
tortured and killed Sandro;*
not even when, face to face
with the President's hit men,
I remained alone.

They eavesdrop on me because they suspect
that I believe in the moment,
that I believe in the land,
in the land and the moment,
in the moment and the land,
in the moment of flint and in the land of firestones,
in the moment of burial rites in the land…
A brief moment—and the poet
will fall to the ground—a moment.

*Sandro Ghirgvliani was brutally murdered by officials of the Georgian Ministry for Internal Affairs in 2006.

—You must not moan but sacrifice yourself!
—You must be killed, so that around the tomb
the sky lights up and the land becomes fertile.
the harvest begins, and in the needle's eye
the Triumphal Arc opens.
A moment immersed in the earth
fecundates the waste land,
to make the earth fertile.
Dignus!

II. Poet – moment. Poet – land (D# minor)

landmomentlandmomentland
momentlandmomentland-
momentlandmomentland-
momentlandmomentlandmoment
moment...

III. Toy Bow (Bb Major)

If just one leaf
flutters on the breeze
autumn has come...

No, I am not intoxicated
by this phrase; I wish only to say
that just one drop fallen
on this parched earth
will give life its victory!

...When a child
they gave me a bow and arrow
and in front of a crowd of neighbours
I turned up in the guise
of Robin Hood, the knight
who requires respect from his friends.
I drew my bow and...
ever since have pursued that arrow.

Following it, I chanced upon you;
it seemed I had already seen you somewhere...

and now, coming across me, you invite me
to stay. I thank you
but how can I if, all my life,
I'm chasing the arrow
I loosed in my infancy?!

And this is my drama,
that I must pursue the arrow
shot into space by the little knight.
Now I am only a simple mortal
and a ham actor
with a white shirt torn over my chest.
From my father's home to my father's home,
this is the trajectory of my arrow.
This is the arrow that will make me
return to my homeland.
I pursue it through forest and vale,
along sidewalks and runways;
gossip and lies rain down on me,
but I ignore them and forge ahead tenaciously
until the sign shows up before me
with the words ITHACA. Welcome!
…Two years ago, along this way
it happened that
I tripped on a marble slab and,
shattered, Christ raised me.
Looking at the slab I read a name,
the dates of birth and of death,
—it was my sister's tomb.

I followed my arrow again
as a Wise Man followed the star
and his joy was without end
when he saw the Virgin holding a Child—
the Mother of God and the daughter of her own son.

In pursuit of the arrow, suddenly
I chanced upon Her—

she had the body of Eve
and the shoulder of a true friend.

At times, they threw knives at my back;
other times, the trolls of the Sovereign;
at times facebook's indecencies,
sometimes utter ignorance, and even
unedited pulp literature.
Both local or foreign editors, you
ask me to stay with you
but how can I betray the arrow
loosed by the hand of a child?

Let me tell you a local playground story:
It was decided to put on Hamlet
at the b-rated secondary school
and when the parts were allotted,
each could choose the one he preferred,
I joined in the representation
dressed as Robin Hood from the other play.

This life choice of mine
has always been the same;
it is my destiny
and so I entered the flow of life
as I did then, in a different play
in the playground show.

P.S.
According to the Constitution
of the Tbilisi playground,
Article 13, clause one:
our playground had its own language,
a universal language,
even more widespread than English,
one that's understood
and is expressed without words.

In this language I breathe and love…
in this language I read books,

in this language I began
the poem that this morning
I titled
The Fertile Land.

IV. Niko Pirosmani (G major)

—Oh, Margarita,
"the dead tree gives no shelter, the cricket no relief,
and the dry stone no sound of water."*
So, I wait for you in April
in the avenue of lilacs, as the lamp
expects its lighting
or the earth a moment,
an officer his medal.
I await you like that man,
just risen from a still warm bed,
who cannot wait to read in the looking glass
or on the window pane
words scrawled in lipstick
—It was amazing! or just
Wow!

*From The Waste Land *by Thomas Stearns Eliot*

Oh, lovely Margarita, I'm grateful
that you showed me the way
from the earth to the heavens,
just as the Chinese master poet
Wang Wei, inspired the symphony
designating a one-way only road
from earth to the heavens.

Draw nearer, in order to enchant the flow,
the sharp blade cuts into the life pulsating in the heart
and fire floods the body—Eve.
Come closer, so I may sow a seed in the furrow
and let the roar of water flood the universe
a babe's cry be heard in the house of birth,
and old glories be restored to the land...
And the water...

the water...
pour it into the cracked furrow.

...The artist's tears fall
on the plastered wall
and, according to the canons of the Byzantine fresco
our good ol' boys line up
by the side of the Ortachala concubines.
—Attention!
—This is the artist Niko Pirosmani,
the icon painter of the local inns.
"The portrait of the actress Margarita."*
—Oils, oilcloth.
—A million dollars, one!
—a million dollars, two!
—Two million!
Two million, one!...

*From "Das Lied von der Erde (The Song of the Earth)" by Gustav Mahler

V. Manifesto (A major)

A spectre haunts Europe,
the ghost of poetry wanders there,
attempting to save the Man
in the citizen.

Our epoch has lost an author;
in the new universe three things are lacking:
—the ladder to the heavens
—the bridge over the sea
—the author for this age.

The "Black Square" of the maestro Malevi—
is a sublime metaphor
between the light and the switch
between the moment and the land,
if you wish, between me and the arrow
that I loosed when a knight.

A spectre haunts Europe,
the ghost of poetry wanders around

to redeem freedom to democracy
so that the Land becomes Homeland,
to tear a verse
from wastepaper
and press a drop of wine
from a cheap bottle.

A spectre haunts Europe...
—"Destabilisation" is a word
that does not go down well in our age
but cannot be spat out.

"Destabilisation"—this word
now sounds like Carthage
and for the successful
has become a shooting target.

This word must be punished
because it is an outsider on the great board
where the mass media has all the means
to transmit in direct how our age
takes leave of its dignity.

A spectre haunts Europe,
the ghost of poetry is lurking—

In Florence, on the Piazza della Signoria,
they poke fun at us, raising a monument composed of shit
—"put your old Renaissance behind you!"—
But when the flies started buzzing around
and it became impossible to breathe
they had to take it down.

A spectre haunts Europe.
Europe goes to vote
as though it were going to mass,
to vote for Barabbas, and then pray to Jesus
to save them from calamity.

The poet's ecclesia is the salt of the earth,
that small number of people

who don't lose their dignity
whatever misfortune befalls them.
The poet's ecclesia is the only supporter
of the word "destabilisation."

Because the mission is to save poetry
and not share anxiety with others,
the poet places himself before ungodliness
as the main target.

—" Defend us, all of you!"—
as though you built the church yourselves"...
cried the wife of the murdered Ilia Chavchavadze,
herself deeply wounded.

You must be killed, so
the price of land around your tomb
rises!

Even here, as elsewhere,
the same thing occurs.
National literature is affected!
National literary pulp is to the fore.

—"Don't think I'm worth nothing!"—
you hear the desperate plea;
more than death in Georgia, the fear
is of being a social bumpkin.

And the Georgian, too, wanders around Europe,
but, unlike the spectre,
he seeks to comprehend, to know what he searches,
what he has lost, before he seeks to understand
who wants him in Europe.

Once a Sultan pulled forth a Yatagan
and severed Byzantium from a drowsy Europe.
He wiped off the blood and hung it
over Istanbul, in the moon's stead.

Since then, antique plaster
flakes from every wall,

and the European tourist
sees Byzantium smiling, like
a father at his son's return.

In the same way, Georgian poetry,
where the mellow Orient fades,
radiates its sublime and antique simplicity.

The wall clock indicates the nineteenth century;
on the Tissot wristwatch, the 6th November of 2020,
a new poetry is being written…
The quill's nib knows
that both are out of kilter.
The universe is trapped in time,
while the poet travels through time.

And he entrusts time
not to the clock's hands,
but to the wings of a sparrow-hawk.
Time, like Columbus,
travels on the poet's voice
in order to discover the man
in a forgotten citizen.

—"Let my people go…"
these are the words you should say
to the old Pharaoh.
Von Karajan took hold of the baton
with which Moses cleft the waters.

The Argonauts moored at the Colchis,
when elections were being held in the capital;
the watchers, headed by Jason,
scanned the votes;
the patriots hid the Golden Fleece,
and on the photo of the Duce painted a halo,
expecting the sky to open.

Just as then, in the house of the Father,
the merchants may be found;
they won't stop futilely sacrificing
for their own personal profit…

"Restless yearnings of moneymaking will not in vain have glowed"
(ho trovato questa frase solo nella versione inglese, non in quella italiana. This phrase was not in the Italian translation, but in the English)

The state looks for a criminal in every man,
Poetry, on the other hand, looks for Adam in the criminal.

A ghost of poetry wanders
along the dusty shelf.
The sun rises in the east
and sets in the west.
Time travels between verses,
going back and forth,
everyone joins up
at the working lunch;
only the poet will not give up
his vehement desire
to save the man in the citizen…
And he wanders around…wanders around,
the ghost of poetry is wandering around.

VI. The fable of the Tailor King (C# major)

I'm an old tailor
and I carry in my pocket a flask of vodka;
although I love to eat baklava,
I'm content with a slice of ham.

Meeting a friend at the market,
we sit around the cask to eat,
and as soon as we raise our morning glasses,
he praises me for my past life.

My faithful drinking buddy
is proud to wear the rags of a tramp…
after a couple of glasses, I am happy
to share a plate of pickles with him.

A third one illuminates every cranny,
sunrise floods the warming body
…and the desire to yield your soul to Christ
…and the wish to slap Death in the face.

As I told you, I was a tailor once,
and I hope to see the angel again.
That old tale of the Fisher King
doesn't tell me anything new.

I launched Eurasian fashion,
I reached the summit of my art,
and on the podium catwalks
I paraded Rachel's lineage.

Only a Tbilisi guide could explain
why Europe and Asia are there arm in arm;
I wouldn't say that of the Brooklyn bridge,
while the Metekhi bridge unites two poles.

Not merely, Europe and Asia, Tbilisi
also links the past to the future;
to let you know how beautiful it is,
I mention the city of my birth.

And in the old quarter of Petkhain
I taught the difference between good and evil;
I dressed the Baptist in a tunic,
and made the cut-out for Christ myself.

I do not know from whom I inherited
But I feel strongly that I am the heir…
the moment I touched the cords
I exclaimed instinctively—AVE EVA!

The moment I touched the cords,
I exclaimed in wonder – AVE EVA!
And from that moment on, I praise
my sweet love in sacred verses.

Bucking the trend of our time,
I repeat the words: AVE EVA!
while she lies on the red carpet,
breast heaving, she becomes
a part of my poetic composition.

Sometimes I doubt: am I still near
or moving away from the Byzantine fresco?
Time is passing me by
or am I passing by it?...
Once again, I draw a sketch
and that time of old returns.

Instead of waiting for the rains,
on my homeland, I let myself drip down.
I am not one who dodges danger,
it's always the risk that protects me.

On the covers of glossy magazines
they publish my photo, to flatter me,
both full face and in profile,
but the beauty of the truth they rejected
I will never deny, even without vodka.

—May the cross protect them, but
to protest holding a cup of coffee
is not, I believe, a true protest,
so I, with a small glass of vodka,
bless what they have denied.
After they destroyed my father's tombstone,
I kicked open the Hotel doors,
because I won't tolerate trade in his house,
nor let Judas Iscariot prevail.

If the judge will not consider
the mass and the prayers,
I'll present him with a divine document
on how to transform words into poetry.

—This is the strength that enforces the logos,
when one has faith,
do you understand, mister?
Words are transformed into poetry
just as water and wine become Christ
...At times, I'm assailed by doubt:
what happened—
did it really happen?

Then the vodka sees to the polishing
of verses into decasyllabic verse.

One moment of life is sufficient
when it falls on the waste land,
to declare
—Noooooo
to the post apocalypse age; I tell you
the truth and swear by the life of that moment.

On a throat parched from a hangover,
if you sprinkle one drop of vodka,
the crowd transforms, becomes people,
and, at times, God is very near…

www.ingramcontent.com/pod-product-compliance
Lightning Source LLC
Chambersburg PA
CBHW011148290426
44109CB00023B/2533